A Day in Court with Mrs. Trinh

written by
ALICE K. FLANAGAN

photographs by
CHRISTINE OSINSKI

Reading Consultant
LINDA CORNWELL
Learning Resource Consultant
Indiana Department of Education

CHILDREN'S PRESS® *A Division of Grolier Publishing*
New York • London • Hong Kong • Sydney • Danbury, Connecticut

Special thanks to Mrs. Trinh for allowing us to tell her story.

Also, thanks to:

Ari	*Diep*
David	*Félice*
Duane	*Dan*
Isabel	*Ernesto Lopez Jr.*

The Legal Aid Society
(New York City)

Author's Note:
Mrs. Trinh's last name is pronounced TRIN.

Library of Congress Cataloging-in-Publication Data
Flanagan, Alice.
   A day in court with Mrs. Trinh / written by Alice K. Flanagan ; photographs by Christine Osinski ; reading consultant, Linda Cornwell.
      p. cm. — (Our neighborhood)
   Summary: Follows a legal aid attorney through her day as she researches a case, pulls together proof, gives her brief to the judge, and speaks for her client.
      ISBN 0-516-20008-9 (lib. bdg.)   0-516-26246-7 (pbk.)
      1. Legal assistance to prisoners—United States—Juvenile literature.
[1. Lawyers. 2. Occupations.] I. Osinski, Christine, ill. II. Title. III. Series: Our neighborhood.
KF337.5.P7F58 1997
344.73'03566—dc21

                                           97-2182
                                             CIP
                                             AC

Photographs ©: Christine Osinski

Meet Mrs. Trinh and her family.
They are Jewish and Vietnamese.

In a few months, Mrs. Trinh will
have her sixth child. She is a busy
wife and mother. She also has an
important job helping others.

Each day, Mrs. Trinh takes two of her children to school. Then she catches the train to the city.

Mrs. Trinh is a
legal aid attorney.

She helps people in jail get a chance to try to prove they should be set free.

If they cannot afford to hire an attorney to help them, the government pays Mrs. Trinh to do the job.

She studies their cases to learn if they have a chance to get out of jail and if she should help them try. That chance is called an appeal. It's everyone's right, even if they're not American.

The people Mrs. Trinh helps are
called clients. Usually, she never sees
them. They are in jails too far away.

But she writes to her clients and talks to them on the telephone.

Mrs. Trinh reads many reports about her clients. Sometimes, she finds proof that mistakes were made, and her clients should not be in jail.

Then she thinks about how she will show the proof to the judges.

Sometimes, it takes a long time before Mrs. Trinh has the proof she needs to give a client a second chance.

16

Then she types the
information in a report.
The report is called a brief.

Mrs. Trinh takes the brief into court.

She gives the brief to the judges . . .

. . . and speaks for her client.

She tells the judges why her client's punishment should be changed. Attorneys for the other side tell why the punishment is correct.

Clerks help the judges and keep the court running smoothly.

What happens next? The judges decide. Usually, there is no change in the punishment.

But sometimes, a person gets out of jail sooner, or a person is even set free.

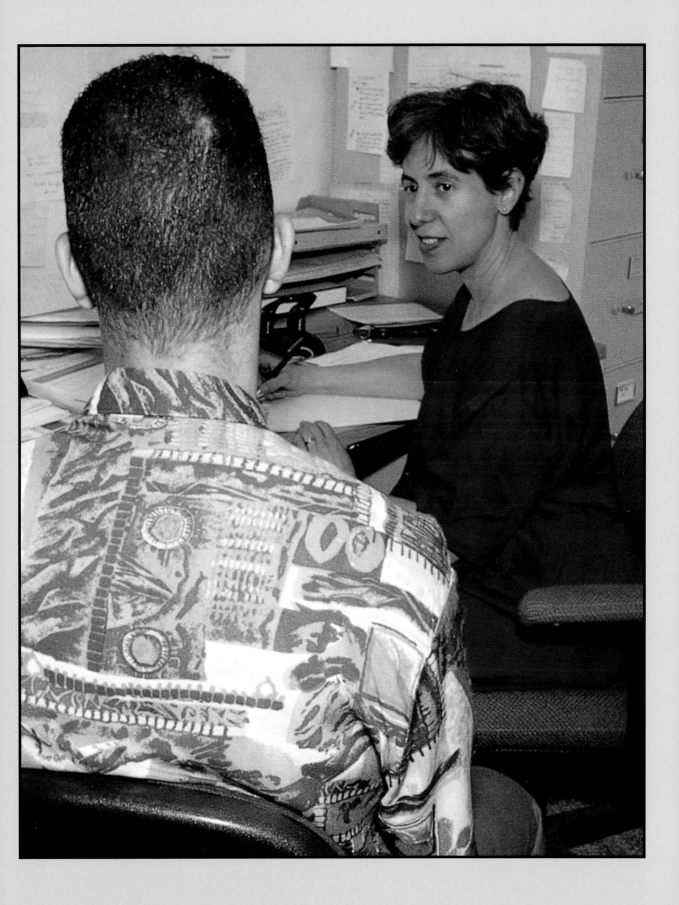

Mrs. Trinh likes being a legal aid attorney.

She helps those who cannot
help themselves.

Without someone like Mrs. Trinh to help people in jail, those who are poor might never get a second chance.

Meet the Author
and the Photographer

Alice Flanagan and Christine Osinski are sisters. They grew up together telling stories and drawing pictures in a brown brick bungalow in a southwest-side neighborhood of Chicago, Illinois. Today they write stories and take photographs professionally.

Ms. Flanagan resides in Chicago with her husband and works as a freelance writer. Ms. Osinski is a photographer and teaches at The Cooper Union for the Advancement of Science and Art in New York City. She lives with her husband and two sons on Staten Island.